"LESSONS"

in

COURAGE

Poems For My Ukrainian Friends

LON WARTMAN

authorHOUSE®

AuthorHouse™
1663 Liberty Drive
Bloomington, IN 47403
www.authorhouse.com
Phone: 833-262-8899

Published by AuthorHouse 09/16/2022

ISBN: 978-1-6655-6717-6 (sc)
ISBN: 978-1-6655-6715-2 (hc)
ISBN: 978-1-6655-6716-9 (e)

Library of Congress Control Number: 2022914478

Print information available on the last page.

Contents

Dedication Page

I dedicate these poems to the people of Ukraine. I am convinced that they will eventually win this war. They are a very strong willed nation fighting for and defending their right to freedom. I sincerely believe in their cause. This is a cause we freedom lovers should applaud.

Poet's Comments/ Foreword/ Introduction

The poems in this collection concern the invasion of Ukraine by Russia and the preservation of a courageous and freedom loving people. It is a collection of sad and dark poems. Poems that I was very reluctant to write. Poems that no one should ever have to write or contemplate writing. The problem is that the invasion of Ukraine by Russia has affected my writing and thoughts. Just as we were toppling the COVID crisis and returning to somewhat of a normal state of being, Russia invaded Ukraine for no apparent reason. They unleashed bombs and missiles of indescribable destruction that have killed thousands of innocent civilians. The horrible atrocities that Russia is inflecting on the people of the Ukrainian nation is tragic and appalling. It is something that never should have happened in this day and age. Hopefully the world will learn from this conflict and that evil can be erased from this planet. However, that is indeed doubtful.

Regardless, I have chosen to write Fifty-one (51) poems that portray my thoughts and emotions about this war. I will pull no punches, my words will stand by themselves. If you are offended by my selection of words, so be it. There is nothing more horrendous than war and the crimes that sometimes go along with it. In essence, I have thrown the usage of slang words into some of these poems for sometimes there is no other way to describe my feelings.

I am impressed by the courage of the Ukrainian people and their leader Volodymyr Zelensky. I am in awe of their willingness to fight and die for their country. I love their national anthem for I believe it embodies the soul and courage of their people. I have portrayed it in full a couple of times and have used some of its verbiage when I felt it added to a poem.

There will be many articles, books, and poems written about this war and the courage of the Ukrainian people. This small book "Lessons in Courage" is something I believe the world needs to understand about a powerful nation invading a much smaller one and the courage it takes to defeat the beast that started it. My central message is that powerful nations can win a war but they cannot win the will of the people they conquer. This is something that no power can take away from them. We Americans know this all too well. Time will eventually tell this story. The world will have to be patient. This is the twenty-first century and, we Sapiens, should know better by now. This world has so much to offer and it is an atrocity that this happening in this day and age. The Ukrainians are pissed and rightly so. I am pissed as well.

A book that inspired some of the poems in this collection is "The Gates of Fire" written by Steven Pressfield. It is indeed a telling story of courage and the strength and will of a people in a war fighting a much more formidable foe. It is a very thought provoking read.

Shche ne vmerla Ukrainas' (Ukraine Has Not Yet Perished)

The glory and freedom of Ukraine has not yet perished
Luck will still smile on us brother-Ukrainians.
Our enemies will die, as the dew does in the sunshine,
and we, too, brothers, we'll live happily in our land.

We'll not spare either our souls or bodies to get freedom
and we'll prove that we brothers are of Kozak kin.

'Shche ne vmerla Ukrainas', the national anthem of Ukraine, has just one verse and one chorus – but it remains one of the world's mightiest patriotic songs.

It was formally adopted less than three decades ago, following the country's independence from the Soviet Union in 1991.

The lyrics of the anthem were written in 1862 by Pavlo Chubynsky – Ukrainian ethnografist, folklorist and poet.

The Ukrainian National Anthem provided by the United States Army Band Library is in the public Domain

"That Day The Music Died"

She waltzed in
Through an open door,
Swung around the room
In two-steps meant for four.
She flipped her skirt up high
And danced on bars and table tops.
Sang songs in multiple keys,
Blew kisses to all the boys.

There was much glee
In this world we
Likened to see.
We were happy and free.
We could be what
We wanted to be.

We journeyed
Around the world.
Ate steak in Timbuktu.
Drank wine in Tuscany.
Sailed across the seas.
We were as happy as
Happy could be.

Then, on a winter's day,
A storm began to brew.
From the East
Came thunder and hail
Lightning and twister tails.
Doors torn open.
Shredded glass on the floors.
Roofs in flames.

Vultures at our gates,
Grasping at our doors.
The music stopped.
The sun went dark.

We cowered
Under table tops
Hid in concrete pits
As little ones clung
To mother's skirts

We wondered why?
Why these vultures at our gates?
Why they chose to steal our lives?
How they forced us to hate
Their unpardonable sins.

There is no glee
In this world we
Likened to be.
No longer happy and free,
To be what
We want to be.

No dancing in bars
Waltzes on a summer's eve
Wine from Tuscany
Sailboats to Timbuktu.
Our homes ravaged.
Our lives raped.
Boys sent to war.
It isn't fair.

Is there no end
To the joys we cannot have?

Our Joys
Flew out the door
That winter's day
When the east winds blew,
The music died.

This poem and several others are a reflection of how I am emotionally tied to the war in Ukraine. We just came through two and a half years of the COVID virus and now we have this unprovoked, war that is once again tearing the world apart. Why, oh why, must we live in a perpetual crisis mode? Beats the shit out of me. Yes, the world has plenty of problems, but nothing like what we see happening in Ukraine. Someday this will all come to an end. However, many lives will have been shattered and much joy and happiness lost. For, WHAT?

"Winters of Discontents"

The many winters of our discontents
Lie in trenches with the dead.
Mothers in pain.
Boys lost in vain.
Nothing plainly gained.

What empire will repent?
Saving souls from Hells bloodied gate.
Piled high in trenches is their fate,
As priests lament their deaths
A crown will not relent.
What cause is there so prodigious?
Slaughters all who differ?
Lays waste to metropolises?
Kills without remorse?

From where cometh this hate?
Through what gate?
What kind of man
Leaves babies seeking breath?
Women without life?
Boys piled high in trenches?

Empires laid to waste,
Many without faces,
Many without places,
All for what?

Pride?
Envy?
Jealousy?

One man...
44 million seek redemption.

Let him
Lie in trenches with the dead.
The many winters of our discontents.

"Don't You Understand"

Without fear or favor
We shall never waver.

This land is ours
Not yours to devour

Try with all your might
You have not the right.

We are the keepers of this land
Don't you understand?

You cannot destroy.
We are not your toy.

Your shallow ideology
It is but forgery.

Place it in your howitzers,
Take a selfie of yourself.

You cannot win
The hearts of our countrymen.

Why don't you understand,
What you misunderstood?

"600 Miles"

The distance not far.
Can be driven by car,
In less than a day.

It struck home
How distant we are,
How different we are.

It couldn't happen here.
But it did happen here.
We couldn't conceive.

That's what we thought.
Mornings kissed by the sun,
Nights lit by the moon.

Nights full of laughter.
Beds sowing love.
Priests speaking peace.

That Thursday day,
600 miles away,
The distance not far.

Ominous clouds rolled in
Full of thunder and fire.
Some of our own kin.

Blue skies turned black,
Yellowing fields brown,
Confusion abound.

Why, you wonder, why.
What for,
You wonder what for.

A man on a mission,
Without a reason,
An obscene obsession.

Always somewhere else,
But not here,
But it is.

Mariupol gone,
Streets full of rubble,
Thousands dead.

What for,
You wonder what for,
It couldn't happen here.

But it did.

The distance not far,
Moscow to Kyiv,
600 miles by car.

Pelosi they screamed.
To the Capitol they stormed.

Stolen elections
They said.
It couldn't happen here.

But it did.
How different are we?
The distance not far.

"Worlds Apart"

Little girl on Sycamore Street
In yellows and blues
Terry cloth hat
Flapping ears
Running and skipping
Twirling and jumping
Laughing out loud
Happy with life

Mother on porch
Smile on her face
Such a pretty girl
So full of Joy
Contented heart
Joy she bequeathed
From seeds within
A gift from her God

Little boy on Mariupol Street
Tattered clothes
Worn out shoes
Bloody nose and bleeding heart
Tripping and falling about
Tears in his eyes
Crying out loud
Starved of life
Mother in doorway
Eyes full of tears
Such a mournful sight
So full of hope

Soul in-contempt
Love she bequeathed
From seeds within
A gift from her God

Two opposites
In worlds apart
A little girl
A little boy
Waiting for life
One of Joy
One of sorrow

Two mothers
In worlds apart
Loving each child
One of hope
One of despair
Tears of Joy
Tears of fear

A little girl from Sycamore Street
A little boy from Mariupol Street
So defined the differences
So tragic the scene
The little girl marries
The little boy dies
The facts of life
In Worlds Apart

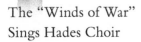

"The Winds of War"

The "Winds of War"
Sings Hades Choir

Sirens in our brains
Sledges on steel
Ringing our ears
Illuminates our fears

Cannons bursting
Base drums beating
Soldiers marching
Babies crying

Torpedoes feed the sky
Lucifer is calling
Visions of Hell
Corrupt the brain

Concrete rubble
Covers our heads
Sonic Booms
Drive us insane

Maestro Lucifer
Commands the choir

It is not "IF"
But "When"

When will "WE" end this song?

"Dare We Compare"

Dare we compare?
Does history tell?
Must we remind those
Who reek of Hell?

900 days...

The siege of Leningrad,
Over 1.5 million starved, frozen or killed.
Is this your legacy?
The blood on your hands
Runs cold.
Yours to behold.

Who was the man
Who struck such hell?
Brought purgatory
To your shores.
Must we remind?

Are you different?
The man you aspire to be?
100,000 marching on Kyiv.
For what?

Make ready your sabers Boys.
Make ready your sabers.

You don't give a s...t
Those you kill
Those you starve
Dead children in the streets

Old men and women
You wish to kill them all
Is there another word for your insanity?

Make ready your sabers Boys.
Make ready your sabers.

They will come
From the far corners
Of the earth.
Freedom fighters.
One million strong,
They will come.

Make ready your sabers Boys.
Make ready your sabers.

Turn the tide you sinful man,
Turn the tide,
Before "YOUR" blood runs cold.

Gaze upon your face
In your crystal ball.
See who you see.
See what happens to thee.

History tells all.
It's coming for you.

Make ready your sabers Boys.
Make ready your sabers.

Your peoples long endured
That siege;
Those 900 days.
You think Mariupol
Not the same?

Turn the page you sinful man.
Turn the page,
Before your blood runs cold.

Make ready your sabers Boys.
Make ready your sabers.

You have a job to do.
Dare We Compare?
I prophesize this for thee.

I believe Mr. Putin needs to be reminded of his Nation's Past. The Siege of Leningrad (St Petersburg today) was one of Hitler's most egregious and horrible acts. (Close behind that of his attempt to exterminate the Jewish population in Europe.) What the Russian people endured during this siege should serve as a reminder of what you should not inflict upon other human beings. Regardless, as to how long the Ukrainians are forced to endure, the end result will most likely be the same. This is a call to all freedom fighters out there to step up to the plate and help the Ukrainians in this most challenging of events being played out for the whole world to see. There is still time, Mr. Vladimir Putin to end this senseless war.

"Spring Time"

The dark days of winter have passed
The snow gone at last.
The cold, a memory forborne.

As the Earth awakens
Will the meadows turn green?
Will the bluebirds sing?
Will the mission bells ring?
Will the cherry trees bloom?
Will mankind repent,
Make way for new dreams?
Will she return to me?

How I long to see
The dark winter of war
Be gone.
The cherry blossoms
Dress the DC mall.
The swallows return to
San Juan Capistrano.

How I long to see
The newness of it all,
The birth of a lamb,
The budding of trees,
The greening of grass.

It is time to seed the earth,
To shake a neighbor's hand,
To repair the hearts and land.

Let it rain spring
Across this land and
In its many hearts.

The Meadows are greening.
The Bluebirds are singing.
The Mission bells are ringing.
The Cherry trees are blooming.

It is indeed a time to celebrate.
It is indeed a time to reflect and repair.

She returns to me
She will return indeed
To the many in need.

The coming of spring and world events are at play in this poem. I continue to pray for the people of Ukraine as they are in such dire need of relief from the war that is terrorizing their country. The question I raise is will spring return in all its glory. Will neighbors once again shake hands? Will Ukraine be repaired and by whom? Spring will definitely come and the grass will once again turn green. The answer of course is that spring will come regardless as to what humans are doing to one another.

"I Cry"

I am saddened by the news today;
My heart is empty,
So many taken,
Through no fault of their own.

I am saddened by the evil today;
My soul is crying,
For those who are dying,
Through no fault of their own.

I am saddened by the evil doers today;
For this unforgivable war,
For the destruction it brings,
Through no fault of your own.

I am saddened by the lies;
Coming from the eastern skies,
For the horror it brings,
Through no fault of your own.

I am saddened by the death today;
For blood let on cobblestones,
Drained from bodies,
Through no fault of your own.

I am saddened by lovers lost today;
For graves must be dug,
Empty holes in your souls are left,
Through no fault of your own.

I am saddened for our hate today;
As we comprehend why,
A tear falls from my eye,
In solitude I cry.

"Return to Me"

Return to Me
That which was lost.

Return to Me
Return to Me

You were stolen away.
I cannot find.
Traces of you are few.

Return to Me!
Return to Me!

I've searched from
Dawn to setting Sun
In darkened alleys
And grassy plains

I've scoured mountains
Vales and forest trails.
Many a stone I've turned

Where have you gone?
Where have you gone?

My life is shattered.
My soul in pain.
My heart adrift in tears.

Return to Me!
Return to Me!

I'll leave the door ajar.
I'm on my knees.
My arms await you please.

I know you're hiding there.

Return to Me!
Return to Me!

Please, Joy
Return to Me.

"Rivers of Blood"

Blood flows from my pen.
In never ending streams

Hate pours from my soul
In thundering waves.

Tears fall from my eyes
In torrential torrents.

My body feels your pain,
My mind your sorrow.

My knees are weak.
I pray for your lives.

Mother Teresa prays.
The world prays,
This hideous hell to end.
I see mother's crying,
Babies dying,
Savages ravaging.

I watch as buildings burn
And factories ruined.
No coming home.

I feel your trembling hearts.
Your despairing eyes.

I hear your mournful cries.
The fear from the skies.
Shock waves of terror.
Unforgivable atrocities.
My heart bleeds.
My soul aflame.

It's him I blame.
My pen runs red.

"My Russian Friends"

Some say you haven't a heart,
    But I say you do.

Some say you haven't a soul,
    But I say you do.

Some say you don't know compassion,
    But I say you do.

Some say you don't know empathy,
    But I say you do.

Some say you don't know truth,
    But I say you do.

Some say you have no courage,
    But I say you do.

Some say you have no morals,
    But I say you do.

Have you wondered,
    Why I say you do?

I say you do because,
    You know love.

Some would say I'm wrong
    But I know.
        I just know.

"My Russian Friends-2"

Do you hear the Finches
Singing in the trees?

Do you see the grass
Greening in the vales?

Do you feel the north bound breeze
Tingling you cheeks?

Isn't it springtime there?
Isn't it time to cast off your fur lined coats?
Isn't it Easter there as well?
Isn't it time for new beginnings?
What are you waiting for?

Don't you hear the thunder in the west?
See the lightening in the sky?

Don't you smell black powder in the wind?
Your boys off to war?

Do you know why?
Do you know the truth?

Aren't your boys coming home dead?
What are you waiting for?

I'm waiting,
I'm waiting for you.

I'm waiting for your springtime.
I'm waiting for you to turn this war around.

I'm waiting to hear the Finches
Sing in my trees.

I'm wanting to dance with you in a
Springtime breeze.

What are you waiting for?

"My Russian Friends-3"

The truth be known,
I am of your blood.

I came from your fields;
Planted "Russian Red" on our Kansas plains

I figure we're still one.
I have no complaints
But one...
"You should have come along."

I know you've seen many wars
And lost many young souls.
I know you've been raped
And plundered,
Pillaged and left dying
On snow covered fields.

But...
      You've never changed.

It is "But" your time to
Leave your hate behind.

It is "But" your time to
Cleanse your soul
Forgive your past
What you are doing
Cannot last... Will not last.

We are but brothers.
Let us show you the path.
Lay down your arms.
Bring your boys home.
Leave your neighbors alone.
Come, be one with us.
You are so, oh so, much better than that.

"Super Powers"

The powers that be
Exemplify

How to lead
How to feed
All in need,

Or

How you bleed
Those who plead
All in need.

It

Defines your destiny,
Refines your respectability,
Requires your responsibility.

Can

Seed your place in history,
Grow you mountains of good,
Harvest you fields of hate.

Rain

Statues of honor,
Manifestos of evil,
Psalms of love,

Or

Devour you in sophistry,
Drown you in hypocrisy,

Or

Baptize you in fonts of peace,
Rivers of trust.

You have to choose,

For if you lose,
Steepled bells will not ring.

"Will of The People"

The one thing we hold dear.
The one thing many fear.

Tis more than an oath.
Tells the strength of your soul.

Tis more than a belief.
It is your life.
It can neither be stolen
Nor broken,
Pissed on
Nor stomped on.

It is neither for savages
To ravage,
Nor thieves
To steal.

Armies have tried.
Many have died.

As hard as
Titanium steel,
The Trident our seal.

It is our pride.
It is our duty.

It is our honor.
It is our will.

The will of our people.
The soul of our country.

"Let's Ban War"

Have your ever thought
About banning war?
How much better we
All would be
If we just banned war?
So much more we could do.
We could buy food
And clothe the poor.

We could tuck our boys
In down filled beds.
Throw away the spade
That dug their graves.
There is so much more we could do.

Build homes for the lost.
It wouldn't be much of a cost.
Tis certainly ours to choose,
For we couldn't lose.
There is so much more we could do.

Let everyone have religion,
If they so care.
Watch news that was good,
Farm fields that would not flood,
If we just banned war.

We could
Heal all the diseases
That kill.
Shut them down

With a needle if we
Had the will,
If we just banned war.

Wouldn't you agree,
How much better
We would be?
Why can't you see?

Little girls could become doctors
And professors as well.
Provide for our mothers
And fathers when aged.
There is so much more we could do.

We could ban guns.
Take them off our streets.
Rid alleys of crime.

I can think of many more,
If we just banned war.

For what is it we do?
Blow holes in walls?
Put refugees on trains?
Fill trenches with dead?
Will we ever get ahead?

It is indeed a crime
Whose time has come.
Open our minds
And let us find,
Fields of clover,
Instead of this grime.

How stupid we are.
How egregious it is.
There is much more good
For us to share,
If we just banned war.

What is happening in Ukraine is driving me insane.... How silly and frivolous it is. A power grab of a neighboring nation threatening the world. People who just want to live at peace. All I want to say is take your tanks back home and leave well enough alone. There are plenty of problems in this world that need our attention and here we sit watching this stupid power grab unfold.... Makes little sense to me.

"I Need Music"

I need music
When my heart is broken
No one there to listen

To make me happy
To dance for joy
When I'm feeling scrappy

I need music
To paint my day
In greens and bluish skies

To make me laugh
To dry my tears
Wash away my fears

I need music
To color the love
I have for you
To drive me home
On star lit nights
When all is quiet

I need music
To love you
In the dark

To dance with you
When we're apart
And cannot whisper
I love you.

I need music to...

I find this war to be very depressing. I also believe that if you are reading these poems you may need a little healing as well.

"I Write These Words"

I write these words
Neither for fame nor glory,
But for the peace
It brings my soul,
That they may touch your heart
In some unbeknownst way.

I write these words
To share my thoughts,
To spread some joy,
That you may enjoy.
Yet, sometimes they are sad.
Yet, I count the days,
When they will once again be glad

I write these words
To entertain you,
To bring a smile to your face,
To help you through your day.

I write these words,
It is my mission,
So that you may know
I write them for you.

"Mariupol, We Used To"

We used to walk along these streets;
Holding hands in the evening hours.

We used to walk among these trees,
As blue birds sang in soft refrains.

We used to stroll through these parks
On Sunday afternoons.

We used to pick flowers in our gardens;
Place them in a vases upon our counter tops.

We used to sing in choirs
While others knelt and prayed.

We used to visit friends,
Play games till way past ten.

We used to laugh and play,
Eat ice cream for our delight
We used to lay in bed,
Make love in the early dawn.

We used to tuck her in bed,
Read her stories of Auntie Anna.
We watched her play hop-scotch
From our front porch step

We used to be happy and gay
Then, they came
And took it all away

"Holes in My Words"

Is what you have destroyed   worth the pain   worth the gain
what are you left with   Are you insane

Will you take care to repair   will you be fair   this nightmare

So many lives have passed   you should have guessed   this
would not last

So many jobs undone who will fill their posts   there is much
work to be done will you pay

Have you made friends   No... Who wants to live in this Hell
Who desires your comradery

So insanely stupid   you ruined their roofs and tore their sheets
your steamy   breath blew them to the street

You stole their loves   You made them run   do your own people
know what you have done

You think they will love you after this   If you do, you are amiss
Their spirits have hardened

Don't you know   you cannot take   what is not yours   You have
created hate for   thousand years

The world has risen   against you   evil has no respect   the
holes in your armor will destroy you

You will learn this lesson   there is no hope in evil   You will soon
see history will not be kind

You could have had so much   If you would have learned from
them   that was not your game

As sad as it may be   you will surely have to pay   I refuse to
mention   your name

Forgive me these holes   My mind amiss   I do not understand

"Vengeance"

My heart is broken
By the winds of this war.
Why this pain
For so little to gain?

What is your desire,
But to kill with fire?

For what is it you lust,
To destroy if you must?

Dare I compare you to "Cronus," *
The master of all evil?
What is the pleasure you seek?
Do you delight in your vengeance?

If vengeance is your intention,
You must delight in this endeavor.

Has "Apate" robbed your soul? *
Lay naked in your bed?
Birthed you daughters of deceit, guile, and fraud?

If you delight in the desecration of a nation,
If you find pleasure in evil,
You must find it entertaining.
I don't...

If annihilation is your pleasure
You must be delighted?
I am not...

To be entertained by evil,
To find pleasure in evil,
Is evil personified
A thousand times over.
You must have dysentery of the brain.
A demented sense of reality.
No rationality.

I leave you now to rot
In your own hedonistic vomit.

- Coronus and Apate are Greek Gods known for their evilness

"Who will Paint This Pain"

Who will paint this pain?
Who is the man,
Who will stand in the rain,
Unveil his passion,
To a world that cannot see?

What canvas will he choose?
What brush will he use?
What blood will he spill?
What strokes will he feel?

Will his hand feel the pain?
Will his mind paint the fear?
Will it be black over red or
Just black on white?

Whose face will he see?
Whose grave will he uncover?
Whose child lies within?
Whose pain will he paint?

Who will be the woman
That paints her motherly pain
For the refugee,
The love of a child lying in a street?

Who will be the Peter Paul Rubens
That reincarnates
"The Massacre of the Innocents?"

What artist will paint the pain?
The pain of starvation.
The pain of thirst.
The retched scent of those
Left rotting in underground vaults.

God forbid
This pain of art,
This masterpiece of criminality,
To hang in some holocaust museum?
Beside the likes of
Salvador Dali's "The Face of War."

Who will paint this pain?
God forgive this retched task.

"Vladimir"

What secrets lie
Within your mind,
That lies cannot define
The transgressions of your soul?

You poison those around,
Lay waste to peaceful lands,
Kill babies with a smile.
You are the Hitler.
Of our times.

Crystal globes foresee
Your life in silhouettes.
Ghostly Spirits
Dancing round the fire
Eating at your flesh
Dust devils boil
From round the feet
Of ancient's chanting
Mournful séances
To your rotting bones

Left alone
On your mighty throne
Father Time is calling.
Calling for your soul.

Can't you taste the fire
Burning up your flesh?

For...
You lost when the first
Cannon fired.

"Leave Us"

Leave us.
Leave us be.
Leave us from this earth.
Of mankind's greatness,
You are not worthy.
You dishonor mankind.
You rank with the shit holes of all time.

You are evil.
You are evil personified.
Your legacy
Forever laid to rest
In a garbage dump of shit.

As maggots gnaw
On your stinking flesh
Can you tell us why?
Why you chose this way
For your fame?

Please leave us.
Please leave us from this earth.
Your name I shall not use.

Oh, how I despise this man, I prefer not to use his name for he is insane. Just how long will the people of Russia put up with this man? It is apparent that the Russian people will become known for their evil, not their goodness. Europe has been relatively peaceful for 75 years. It was in the palm of your nation's hand to live in peace with the world and he blew it. He took his wrath out on an innocent people for no apparent good reason. As the Russian boys come back in body bags I'm sure they will understand that evil never wins. I believe you are much better than this. Remember, Judgment Day is nearer than your think. Again, you the people of Russia, you are so much better than this.

"Ramifications"

You stole our tractors.
Now what?

You took our grain.
Now what?

You hold our farmers hostage.
Now what?

You destroyed our ports.
Now what?

You devastated our steel mills.
Now what?

You destroyed our villages.
Now what?

You say you want this land?
Now what?

Who will own this land?
Now what?

Who will farm our fields?
Who will rebuild our homes?
Who will repair our factories?

An easy task.
You would take over.

No it wasn't.

Now What?
Do you have the will?
Do you have a plan?
Has anyone ever told you that missiles can't grow wheat?
That we are not your slaves.

"What are You Going To Do?

If you conquer
Will you repair?
Or
Plunder at will

Will you make
Them one of you?
Or
Drown them in the sea

Will you protect
The young, the old.
Or
Turn them into slaves

Will you let them
Live without fear?
Or
Fear for their lives

Will you give them homes?
Will you give them jobs?
Or
Let them peddle in the streets

What is your plan?
Or
Are you so foolish
As to not have one?

"Consequences"

After the acrid scent of war is gone
And all the bodies buried,
What will you do?
Who will have won?

We'll leave to history
To tell its fate.
The many lost souls and lives
Will live forever in our minds.

How shamelessly your cannons fired,
Laying waste to cribs and schools,
Stations of aid and baptismal fonts.

What monument will you rise
Proclaiming your cowardly will?
On whose soil will it stand?
Who will be most proud,
With nothing to hide?

Such is this repugnant scene.
To the victor belongs the spoils.
How obscene.
No one wins.
To claim victory is but a dream.

Your thieving schemes
Will be revealed.
Your cowardly ways
Will come undone.

Hearts you cannot win.
Our minds resolute.
Our freedom,
Your albatross.

The consequences
Of your machinations
Will bring prosecutions.
"Jus ad bellum"

Vacant Responsibilities"

Some say,
To the victor
Belong the spoils.

The question begs:

Who will clean the
Stone and steel
Piled high on Mariupol's streets?

Who will rebury the dead left
In backyard trenches?

Who will house the
Orphans left on bloodied streets?

Who will rebuild the factories,
Repair the homes,
Rebuild the hospitals,
Open the schools?

Yours to claim.

"Fait Accompli"

Who do I dare
Compare thee to?

Upon whose wall
Will you be hung?

What fame
Will adorn your frame?

What quests
Upon your Crest?

An audacious task
To be a likened to.

Attila the Hun,
            Lenin,
                    Hitler,
                            Stalin,
                                    Pol Pot... Now you

Telling marks of history.
The cesspool of mankind
Summons you.
An unmarked grave
Your stinking bones
Cleansed by maggots
For none to see
                    "Fait accompli"

"Maria"

My Dear Maria:
Would you have ever believed,
That you would have conceived
A Lucifer in your womb?

You, who survived Leningrad,
Know the Hell it was.
The Millions starved,
The Millions dead.

Would you ever desire
His blood to be of yours?

We beg of you to return;
Come back in his midnight dreams
As he slumbers in ice cold sweat.

Follow him on his hollowed rounds
Through the castle he commands

Whisper in his ear,
"You are of my blood,"
Of proud Russian blood,
Of blood that says you are wrong.

Speak to him of this evil,
The Hell he will endure,
The ghosts that will sojourn,
Through his brain in dark refrains.
Their mournful waling soon
Driving him insane.

Dear Mother of Vladimir,
Speak to your son in his midnight hours.

Maria Ivanovna Putina is believed to be the mother of Vladimir Putin. She died in 1998 at the age of 98, one year before Vladimir became Prime Minister of Russia. She survived the siege of Leningrad in WWII.

"What Mothers Want"

I want to wake each day,
To the beauty of this world,
To bask in the serenity of peace.
I want to walk my kids to school each day,
Give them a wonderful home
Without worry of hate and war.

I want to talk to my love each day;
Whisper words of romance and happiness,
Not how we can survive.

I want to open my windows each day;
Let the springtime air fill my home,
Not to the scent of munitions spent.

I want to pray each day,
This war to end,
Not to the death I see

I want to hope each day;
We discover a way
To return to our ways
I want to find the courage each day,
To fight the rage inside,
We no longer have to hide.

I want to find the will each day
To destroy this evil
Inflicted upon us.

I want to find forgiveness each day,
If there is such a word,
For the thieves of our souls
Who left the dead in our streets.

I want to find your help each day;
To keep us alive
In our hour of need.

I plead...

"I Could Be"

The wind is howling.
The forests are burning.
People running.
I think I'm in Hell.
But,
I could be in
Mariupol,
Where it
Really is
HELL.

"This Thing"

Ancient scribes have asked
What is this thing?
What is this word?
What gives it life?

Speak to us this word
From where doeth it come?
What does it mean?

Tell us of trials that make it so,
Of fires kindled,
Of mountains conquered,
Of plagues revoked,
Of gardens born?

When spears are thrust
For what is wrong.
Who be the one
Who speaks unjust?

When words are hissed
Who proclaims enough
To the one who retched
Those vile words?

When history is writ
Who be the one
Who kissed the nails
On the cross?

Who are these men
Who stand alone?
Are duty bound?
From where doeth it come?

It comes from those
Who know the many doors of wrong.
Those who know the hands of good.
Those who know duty and responsibility.
Those who do not ask.
Those who just know.

It resides within.
Is the heartbeat of their souls.
Their passion for love.
Their understanding of time.

They know neither when nor if
Time will call for them.
Neither when nor if
It will be their time.

But,

They are prepared.

Are You?

Who will write your history?
Will you be the man or woman?
Who has the courage?
To be courageous?

Will it be your time?
Or, is time calling you?
You must know courage.
That is the thing.
You must give it life.

"Courage"

Douse the fear my friend,
Douse the fear.
Tis a dangerous thing my friend,
Tis a dangerous thing.

Awaken the lion inside my friend,
Awaken the lion.
Don't let him slumber my friend,
Don't let him slumber.

Appease your soul my friend,
Appease your soul.
You'll know not peace my friend,
You'll know not peace.

A task that must be done my friend.
A task that must be done.
It will make you whole my friend,
It will make you whole.

You've scribed your place in history my friend.
You've scribed your place in history.

You released the lion inside,
Stood up to the forces of evil.

An indomitable task my friend,
An indomitable task.
It had to be done my friend,
It had to be done.

It made you whole.
Your people followed.
Without a doubt,
You did it my friend,
You did it.

Raise high your flag my friend,
Raise high your flag.
We're so proud my friend,
We're so proud.

We honor you my friend.
We honor your courage,
Volodymyr Zelenskyy

"Over My Dead Body"

We shall not allow
Your armor to pierce our soul.
We are a nation of great men
Who will lay down our lives
For the freedoms we enjoy,
For the love of our land.

Cast any doubt you have
Into a sea of wayward thoughts.
Your destiny decreed by your
Dead soldiers lying in our streets.
Their mothers not knowing
Where they lie.

No matter the days,
No matter the years,
You will not gain the love
Or our land,
The minds of our people.

You are destined for Hell
For what you have tried to steal.
Your blood we'll drain into
The blackest of seas.
Your heart we'll squeeze
When you're on your knees
For there is nothing to please

Return your boys
To their mothers who cry,
Not knowing where they lie.

Before the buzzards pick at their bones.
And devour their eyes.

We stand here
Ready to die.
For the freedoms we enjoy
The love of our land.
Defend we will
The heart and soul of our land.

It takes courage to say these words but even more to carry them to the battlefields. Try as they might great nations can never overcome the will of a strong people whom they are trying to subdue. My own America knows this quite well.

"Bravery, Therapy for My Soul"

How often does reluctance
Muddy the trail
Down which we journey.

Often it is the unknown,
Perhaps evil,
More likely fear.

Admired is the man
Who conquers fear;
Stands above all others
With sword and spear

Commands the brigade
That challenges the foe
Who wishes him dead.
Tis not a charade.

Poetic words often
Find no page
Upon which to sit.
They lie in cages,
Their souls enraged,
Seeking men who will speak,
Thrusting their heads to the ax.
They know not pain,
Have nothing to gain,
Reticence not their game.
The bravest of all,
Men like Volodymyr Zelenskyy,
We lay down Alms.
Tis therapy for my soul.

"Last Stands"

From Thermopylae
To Mariupol.
From the Alamo
To Singapore.

Ages Past have honored
These stands,
Laid wreathes upon
Their graves,
Sang songs in their memory,
Scripted verses of mankind's bravery.

There is much to be said
For these fearless men and women,
Their moral obligations
As sacrificial lambs.

Though they often lose
The battlefield,
They win the war
Of the soul.

As you stand on your rubble,
Raise high your yellow and blue.
Take your oath to a man
Never to be defiled.

Many words will be writ
Of your fearless courage.
History will treat you with
Respect and reverence.

Raise high your yellow and blue.
Raise high your yellow and blue.

"Souls and bodies we'll lay down."

"What Do We Have to Lose"

Will you stand to the last man?
Cause "Freedom" don't mean nothing
Without a fight.

Are you willing to pay the price?
Cause "Freedom" don't mean nothing
If it's free.

Will it come with some blues?
Cause "Freedom" don't mean nothing
Unless it's got some soul.

Will it grant me rights?
Cause "Freedom" don't mean nothing
Without some rights.

Can we share it with our neighbors?
Cause "Freedom" don't mean nothing Baby
Unless you pass it along.

What do we have to lose,
If we aren't free?

My thanks to Janis J. and "Me and Bobby McGee" for some of these thoughts. On the flip side I must say that "Freedom" ain't free even when you have nothing to lose. As the world watches we have a lot to lose.

"The Freedom Tree"

Do you know what freedom is,
What freedom really means?
Are you trapped in a scene
Like a bear in a snare?

The bell of freedom rings
For those willing to lay down their
Hearts and souls.
To hang from a timber
Before they become old.

Many have sought,
But few have found,
The "Freedom Tree."

It is a solitary tree
Hidden in a forest of many trees.
A tree of many branches
And tangled roots.
It foresees the future,
Tells of the past.
Inscribed on its trunk are many lines.

The right to think and speak.
The right to learn and teach.
The right to buy and sell.
The right to come and go.
The right to believe and marry.
The right to own your body.
The right to be what and who you are.

The right to not be tread upon.
The right to punish if done harm.
The right to elect leaders of your clan.
The right to a life you desire without dictation.
The right to a life you desire without retribution.

A sip of nectar from the freedom tree
Is dopamine for the soul,
An aphrodisiac for the heart.
The taste so sweet you'll never retreat.
It grows in your bowels,
Is a flame in the dark of night.

I say go to the forest
In search of that tree.
When it is found
Take another along.
Plug it when its saps runs down.
Share it with your neighbor
On your journey home.

"Ploughs or Stones"

If you had your choice
Which would you chose?

Tilling the soil
Or
A marker for your life.

A lover's grace
Or
Grass covering your face.

He's sending you to war.
You have a choice.
You have to chose.

Do you understand
This gun in your hand?

Do you know if it is right
This war that you fight?

Did they tell you why
Without any lies?
Be it for one man's might
To his sole delight.

I ask these questions
Of you young man,

For you should know
That what you're doing
Is not right.
Tomorrow you'll see
If you live to be.

You had a choice.

I wrote this poem for the young innocent Russian conscripts. They appear to neither know why, or what, or for whom they wreck this horrendous havoc.

"Stay Strong"

I'm with you.
My heart bleeds.
My soul aches.
I feel your pain.

You stand alone,
A beacon on a rocky shore,
Shining bright for freedom's right,
Fighting battles for humanity.

You are strong,
Much stronger than I.
I honor your fight.
It is your right.

Your courage,
Beyond compare,
A cross to bear,
Lives beyond time.
Well beyond mine.

"Honor"

I Honor you Volodymyr,
Your image imbedded in my brain.
Your courage I honor.
I have no words
For the man you are.

Great men have graced
The pages of this earth.
Even before Christ,
Man has conquered fear
And retribution.
Stood above others
Of indisputable fame.

For the man you are
I'll enshrine from afar
Valor your name
Courage your fame
You are the man Volodymyr.

"I Write of This Pain"

I write of this pain
For it is how I feel.
I feel for these people
In their most trying hours.

I write of this pain
For I fear for these people.
I desire them to be strong.
To fight with all their might.
The right to be free.

I write of this pain
To change the world,
The way we see,
Why mothers cry,
And little ones die

I write of this pain.
The insanity of it all.
We are humans who
Think and feel.

I write of this pain
As I wonder why.
Why we are this way.

I write of this pain
And cry
For the many lost souls

I write of this pain
And pray
These rivers of blood
To dry.

I write of this pain
For the world to see,
For the world to feel,
These word I hate,
For they are not I.

I write of this pain
For I know not
What else to do.

The Refugee"

She stood naked
as the soft sprinkling of
water cascaded down
her war torn body.

The scent of concrete dust
still in her veins.
The sound of bullets still
ricocheting through her brain.
Black powder on her skin.
The long frozen road.
The nights without sleep.
Her baby in tow.
The raping of her soul.

Running for life,
Away from the fight.
Leaving footprints in the snow.
Bloodied glass on her kitchen floor.

Her tears poured
as the water caressed
her tired body
washing away those sins.

A bar of soap
will never erase.
A fountain of warmth
will never reclaim.

She somehow survived
those evil men.

Reflecting the life she led
before they came.

The warm water
streams down
her naked body.

"Who Do We Hold Responsible"

This question must be asked
As it has been
For centuries on end.

When man first conceived thought
Did he take,
Or did he partake?

When man first spoke
Did he lie
Or lead others astray?

When man first saw beauty
Did he steal it away,
Not rape as he may?

When man first felt love,
Did he conceive a child
With the woman she was?

When man first felt hate,
Did he pick up a stick
And strike at will?

When man first knew God,
Did he fall on his knees?
Did he define for all?

Did man conceive God
Or
Did God conceive man?

Who is right and
Who is wrong?

Depends on whose side
A man is on.

So,

Who do we hold responsible
For mankind's acts?

"Healing"

There will come a day
When the stratospheres
Of stars and galaxies collide
And our world is calmed.
When kings and queens
Quiet their anger.

When rainbows paint the sky
And babies no longer cry.

When boys and girls
Play in our streets.

When guns are laid aside
And teardrops dried.

When hope returns
And peace is learned.

Only then
Will we heal.
When our nation heals,
The world will heal

We can only hope.

"Dear God I Plead"

I've written about it many times before.
Sang in choirs for the dead.
Laid wreaths upon their graves.

Yet nothing's changed.
Legions of crosses cover the plains.
Prayers never bring them home.

Such a sad world we are.
Power doesn't mean
You are free to war.

It is but time to
Bury all wars.

Dear God,
I plead,
Vanquish war from this world.

"What is My Purpose?"

I write about war.
I write about violence.
It pains me so.
I'm dark inside.
I write about Joy.
I'm happy inside.
To know Joy is to know war and violence.
I want to write more Joy.
It pleases my soul.

"A Cherished Word"

Dark days cloud my vision.
How I see through all this mist
I cannot explain.

How people survive,
Through warring Hells,
Is beyond my comprehension

The struggle,
The pain they endure;
What drives them on
Is mankind's sole treasure.

How people succeed,
The truth they define,
The happiness they find,
Whatever it is they seek.

The most cherished word of all.
Надія
Only man knows this word.

The most important word in all languages.
Hope

Please note that Надія is the spelling of Hope in the Ukarianian language
Hope, is one of the most cherished words in all languages. It is one of
the most sacred attributes of the human species. Hope surrounds us and
embodies us in all that we do. What is there without Hope?

Souls and Bodies We'll Lay Down"

Ominous clouds have
Invaded my soul;
Thrust swords into my heart.

Darker than the midnight sky.
Stars gone forever more.
Bloodied hands in my dreams.

I dream not of tranquility
But of lightning and thunder,
Pain and hunger.

I pray for your peace,
Your hope and honor.
For blue skies and golden wheat.

I pray that your Trident,
Strikes the heart of evil,
Brings this aberration to its knees.

Father, Son and Holy Ghost,
I beseech thee please
Save them from this hell.

May your anthem be sung
By all the peoples,
Of all the nations,
Of this world.

I leave you with this heart felt National Anthem of the Ukraine Nation

National Anthem of Ukraine

In Ukrainian Alphabet
'Shche Ne Vmerla Ukrainas'

Ще не вмерла України і слава, і воля,
Ще нам, браття молодії, усміхнеться доля.
Згинуть наші вороженьки, як роса на сонці.
Запануєм і ми, браття, у своїй сторонці.

Душу й тіло ми положим за нашу свободу,
І покажем, що ми, браття, козацького роду.

(English Translation)
'Ukraine Has Not Yet Perished'

The glory and freedom of Ukraine has not yet perished
Luck will still smile on us brother-Ukrainians.
Our enemies will die, as the dew does in the sunshine,
and we, too, brothers, we'll live happily in our land.

We'll not spare either our souls or bodies to get freedom
and we'll prove that we brothers are of Kozak kin.

The Trident Symbol

I believe the anthem of the Ukrainian Nation is a very powerful poem/song. The chorus says it all. "We'll not spare either our souls or bodies to get freedom." It definitely portrays the courage and tenacity of the Ukrainian people. They aren't going to give up and should not. Their dead soldiers are martyrs for democracy and freedom. They are setting examples of how much they love their freedoms.

Author's Final Comments

Just what is Courage? Is it to stand against evil when all say you shouldn't? Is it the ability to stand up against wrong when most do nothing? Is it the man, is it the woman, who rises above all others and leads by example knowing full well they may not survive? I believe it is a profound sense of duty for the welfare of your fellow human beings that propels one to sacrifice everything he or she has for the good of the whole. In this instance, in this war, it is a battle for a freedom loving people willing to sacrifice all they have for the right to choose their own destiny. May the world learn from their courage.